MW01378113

Made in United States
Orlando, FL
18 December 2023

41239091R00075